Luka Doncic

A Biography of an NBA Superstar

Adrian Almonte

Table of Contents

Introduction 1

Chapter 1: Early Life and Childhood 7

Chapter 2: Making It to the Pros 10

Chapter 3: Entering the NBA Draft 14

Chapter 4: Career Highlights and Achievements.....16

Chapter 5: What's Next for Luka? 58

References 61

Introduction

"He can control a game."

Those are the words of LeBron James when asked to describe the rising superstar Luka Doncic. LeBron is considered by many fellow players, peers, media personalities, and fans around the world as the Michael Jordan of this generation. So, any opinion that he gives on the world of basketball certainly has some merit. And to give credit to a player so young and so early into his playing career is definitely not something to scoff at.

Luka Doncic grew up with basketball in his blood. His father was a former professional player and is currently a coach as well. Even early on, Luka was exposed to the game in such profound ways. This early exposure gave him an advantage in developing his skills and sharpening his talent for the game. Even before he stepped foot on an NBA floor, Doncic was already racking up the YouTube views on video highlights of himself absolutely demolishing his opponents in the EuroLeague as a teenager. The 19-year-old Doncic dominated people who were much bigger and more experienced than he was on the way to winning the EuroLeague MVP and the championship.

It was only a matter of time before the Slovenian phenom would eventually make his way over to the most competitive fish pond in the world of basketball: the NBA. Even though he has only been in the league for four short years, he has managed to rack up a number of accolades, awards, and records that will forever cement his legacy as an all-time great. And that's really saying something for a 23-year-old kid who is still working his way into his prime years. Even LeBron James can't deny that Luka is a generational talent, and the rest of the world should take notice.

Part of the reason why Luka is continually mesmerizing the NBA fandom is because he's such a deceptive talent. He stands at around six feet, seven inches tall. He's not the leanest or the most muscular guy in the league, with a playing weight of around 230 pounds. He looks like a kid because he is one. And he doesn't look like the kind of guy that would be able to outrun, outjump, or outlift anyone else in the NBA. Yet, despite all of this, Luka won the Rookie of the Year award, has led the NBA in triple-doubles in a season, has been an All-NBA First Team selection, and, most recently, has led his underdog Dallas Mavericks team all the way to the Conference Finals of a loaded Western Conference. And the scariest thing about Luka's NBA journey is that it's just getting started.

Doncic is such a special talent because despite everything that he lacks in athletics and physique, he makes up for in intelligence and natural game sense. He has a strongly developed basketball instinct that allows him to outplay and outmaneuver his opponents on the court on a consistent basis. When asked about what it's like to be a scorer in the NBA, Luka simply replied, "It's easy." The NBA is a league that's filled with the best basketball players in the world. And Luka isn't just another boy among the crowd. He's a man-eating lion who's looking to devour anyone who gets in the way of his lofty basketball goals.

Every NBA player is capable of making an impact on the game in certain respects. Some players are terrific shooters who specialize in just putting the ball into the basket. Other NBA players impact a game through their defense by making it harder for their opponents to score. Some players impact the game through rebounds, assists, pace of play, and even by just cheering on the sidelines. But there are a select group of players in the NBA who manage to impact the game in a variety of different areas. Aside from being unstoppable scorers, they can set their teammates up for easy baskets themselves. Aside from controlling the pace of the game, they can rebound the ball and immediately look to make a play on the other end of the court. That's exactly the kind of player that Luka Doncic is. What makes him so hard to stop is the fact that he's very effective in multiple aspects of the game. And while there are many who still criticize his defensive prowess, it's worth noting that he is a young player who is still learning the ropes. It can be easy to take this kid for granted, considering that he was so close to winning the league MVP award in just his second year.

Doncic has good size for his position, and his offensive skillset is so incredibly polished that he looks like he's been playing in the league for decades. Many people have compared him to NBA legends Larry Bird, James Harden, and even LeBron James himself. But there's something unique about Doncic's play that makes him his own man. He has the intelligence and the basketball savvy that made Larry Bird and LeBron James so effective. But he also has the shooting touch and the finishing ability that made James Harden practically unguardable during his prime. Even at such a young age, Doncic already has a basketball IQ that rivals the game's most experienced veterans. A lot of that is influenced by the fact that Doncic was already destroying veterans in the EuroLeague as a teenager.

In this book, we are going to delve deeper into the life of Luka Doncic and every important detail and milestone that has led him to where he stands right now. We are going to touch on his early life and childhood in Ljubljana, Slovenia. This book will talk briefly about what it was like for him to grow up with a former professional basketball player as a father and a strong businesswoman as a mother. This phase of his life touches on Luka's interest in the field of athletics and how he eventually settled on basketball as his primary sport of choice. From there, we can move on to Doncic's first tastes of competitive organized basketball with Union Olimpija. This phase of Luka's life was very important in his development as an athlete and basketball player. It was during this stage that he was able to prove to himself and to others that he had an aptitude for the game and that he was just built differently than other people.

Then, we will dive into Doncic's jump into the pro leagues as a 13-year-old. Fresh off his turn into teenagerhood, Doncic signed a five-year contract with Real Madrid's under-16 squad. It was there that he started to blossom as a basketball player who could really showcase his dominance consistently on the hardwood against other notable talents. For the rest of his teenage life, Doncic dominated the European basketball scene, racking up awards and championships left and right. He propelled himself to a legendary status at such a young age and managed to command the attention of scouts from around the world, including the NBA.

It didn't take long before Doncic himself realized that he could make a dent in the NBA despite never having played organized basketball on American soil before. At 19 years old, Luka entered the NBA draft, and this phase marked the biggest jump in his basketball career so far. While there were many who were skeptical about how Doncic's play would fare against actual NBA players, Doncic was quick to put the critics to rest with a dazzling rookie year that saw him winning the Rookie of the Year award by a landslide. This book will delve into a year-by-year account of Doncic's short career so far and the notable milestones that he has achieved along the way. Even though he's only 23 years old and has only been playing professionally in the NBA for four years, Doncic has already had a career that many other NBA players in history can only dream of.

Of course, even though Luka Doncic eats, sleeps, and breathes basketball, he does have a life beyond the sport. We will take a brief and insightful look into his family life and what Doncic typically does when he's not in a jersey and shorts. From there, we can take a closer look into the career that Doncic has built for himself so far and speculate on the kind of career that he may eventually grow to have in the future.

Usually, when a player is dubbed as a generational talent, they are typically well into their late 20s or early 30s with a formidable body of work to showcase. But that's what makes Doncic so special as a player. The man isn't even 25 yet and he has still managed to somehow take the basketball world by storm. Many consider it a privilege to watch him play at this point of his career when he's still young and developing his raw talents. Only time will tell just how good this talent can truly be once it's all said and done.

Chapter 1: Early Life and Childhood

On February 28, 1999, one of the biggest basketball talents to have ever come out of Slovenia was born in the nation's capital of Ljubljana. Even at an early age, Luka was already exposed to European basketball at the highest level due to the influence of his father Sasa. The older Doncic is a professional basketball coach whose last coaching stint was with the Ilirija team in the Premier Slovenian Basketball League, which is also known as the Liga Nova KBM. Unfortunately, things didn't work out between Sasa and Luka's mother Mirjam Poterbin, who was an owner of a chain of beauty salons. The couple eventually filed for divorce in 2008, with Luka's mother gaining custody and legal guardianship over Luka.

Even before he turned a year old, Luka already showed an aptitude for the game. Close friends and family say that Luka was already touching a basketball when he was just seven months old. His parents gave him a miniature hoop to play with when he turned one and this essentially sparked his lifelong love affair with the game.

However, as Luka was growing up, he also developed an interest in other sports. He was a very athletic child and showed immense skill in most sports that he tried, including soccer, a very popular sport in his country. He would later on be forced to quit the sport because of his growth spurt, which put him at a disadvantage to smaller, nimbler, and quicker players. Luka eventually turned this into a blessing by focusing on a sport that welcomed height and size: basketball.

In an interview with a European basketball media outlet back in 2018, Ms. Poterbin opened up about her son and his passion for the game. Luka's mother described him as a lovely child who always had a lot of energy. She claimed that, as Luka was growing up, he had to channel all of his energy into a variety of different sports. But it was only when he started playing basketball that she noticed a change in his personality and demeanor.

Doncic got his first taste of organized basketball when he was seven years old. Even when he was just starting out, Doncic was faced with the gargantuan task of having to compete with people who were three years older than him. His age and size put him at a disadvantage against his bigger and older opponents. It was this adversity that forced Luka to make up for his physical disadvantages with basketball smarts instead. He developed his playmaking ability at an early age, and this enabled him to become one of the smartest and most calculated players on any court he plays on.

Early on, as Luka got more serious about playing basketball, he started paying attention to the playing styles and techniques of the best players in the world. Growing up, Luka greatly admired Vassilis Spanoulis during his teenage years and was greatly influenced by his play. The Greek basketball star's physical brand of basketball carried over to Luka's style of play as well. Doncic was so enchanted by Spanoulis that he ended up sporting the number 7 when he joined Real Madrid's EuroLeague team. He would carry this number with him into the NBA as well where he currently sports the number 77 for the Dallas Mavericks. On the other side of the Atlantic, Doncic was also paying close attention to the developments in the NBA, wherein he looked up to the world's biggest basketball stars, especially Lebron James.

Chapter 2: Making It to the Pros

At the ripe age of 16 years old, Luka Doncic became the youngest player to ever suit up for Real Madrid in the ACM. The team only granted the youngling two minutes of playing time, but he made the most of it by sinking his only three-point attempt of the game. The team would limit his playing time for the five games that he played during the 2014-2015 season to just a little under five minutes per game. Despite the minimal playing time, Doncic still averaged 1.6 points and 1.2 rebounds as a teenager against full-blown professionals who had been playing the game competitively for years.

It wasn't until the 2015-2016 season that Doncic would really get a chance to prove himself in the big leagues. Real Madrid pushed him up to the senior team and he made his debut in the EuroLeague in October as a 16-year-old. Doncic once again made history by becoming just the 21st player to ever play in the EuroLeague before turning 17. He would have his breakout game against a Gipuzkoa squad with a stat line of 10 points and 4 rebounds. Just a month after, he recorded a season-high 15 points, 6 rebounds, and 4 assists in a matchup against Bilbao. This performance led to Doncic notching the record for the most scored points and the highest Performance Index Rating (PIR) for players under 17 years of age. Doncic would play a total of 39 games for that entire ACB season, and he had averages of 4.5 points, 2.6 rebounds, and 1.7 assists. In 12 games in the

EuroLeague, Doncic averaged 3.5 points, 2.3 rebounds, and 2 assists per game.

While he didn't exactly post stellar numbers, Doncic certainly caught the attention of a number of players and spectators with his polished play despite being so young. It wouldn't be until the 2016-2017 season that the rest of the world would start to take notice of his talents. During a game in early December, Doncic notched 23 points and 11 assists against Montakit Fuenlabrada. His efforts earned him his first ACB Player of the Week award. A few days after that, Doncic scored a team-high 17 points in a victory against Zalgiris Kaunus in the EuroLeague. Doncic continued to dazzle with consistently productive outings in the EuroLeague, and he was even named the MVP of the Round. This made him the youngest player to have ever achieved such a feat.

In the next round, Doncic secured the MVP of the Round honors once again, while sharing it with two other players. Just a couple of days after that, he won the award once more as he led his Real Madrid team to a slot in the EuroLeague Final Four. After playing 42 ACB games that season, Doncic improved his averages to 7.5 points, 4.4 rebounds, and 3 assists per game. His EuroLeague averages were 7.8 points, 4.5 rebounds, and 4.2 assists. After an impressive showing throughout the entire year, Doncic was awarded the EuroLeague Rising Star via a unanimous vote, and he also won the ACB Best Young Player Award.

Even though Luka had already proved himself to as an important figurehead within the EuroLeague and ACB, not many were convinced that would be able to take his game to the next level. At the start of the 2017-2018 season, Doncic would get his shot at proving himself, as Real Madrid's star player Sergio Llull suffered a torn ACL. The young Doncic was now tasked with having to carry the team on his broad but inexperienced shoulders. Doncic gave an underwhelming performance in his season debut by scoring just 8 points, 6 rebounds, and 4 assists. But just a few days later, Doncic went on to score a career-high 27 points in his first EuroLeague game for that season in a winning effort against Anadolu Efes. Just a couple more days after that, Doncic almost notched a triple-double against a powerhouse Valencia team with a stat line of 16 points, 10 assists, and 7 rebounds. On October 24, Doncic bagged the EuroLeague MVP of the Round honors after a powerful performance consisting of 27 points, 8 rebounds, 5 assists, and 3 steals.

The young Doncic had proven that he was more than capable of leading a team as Real Madrid continued to make waves in the ACB and EuroLeague. On May 20, Doncic successfully led Real Madrid to the EuroLeague finals and dragged his team across the finish line for a championship. Doncic was awarded with the EuroLeague Final Four MVP and the EuroLeague MVP. This made him the youngest MVP in league history after averaging 16 points, 5 rebounds, and 4 assists across 33 games that season. Aside from his EuroLeague accolades, Doncic earned the ACB

Best Young Player and MVP awards as well. Toward the end of June 2018, Doncic parted ways with Real Madrid and decided that it was time to take his talents to the NBA as he declared for the draft.

Chapter 3: Entering the NBA Draft

A typical NBA draft class is usually composed of a pool of players who are coming out of college careers around the United States. The top prospects for the draft are usually those who show immense potential when it comes to being ready for the pace and talent of the NBA game. It's very rare for a player in the draft to already have professional playing experience, but that's exactly what Luka Doncic was. However, various NBA scouts and analysts were still concerned with whether or not Luka's talents would translate well to playing in the NBA. After all, Luka lacked the usual agility, speed, and athleticism that most of the other players in the draft pool already had.

With the first pick of the draft, the Phoenix Suns selected DeAndre Ayton. For the longest time, the NBA had been a league dominated by guards and forwards who were athletic and skilled enough to cover most of the floor. Ayton was a throwback big man whose game relied a lot on post-ups, pick-and-rolls, and back-to-the-basket moves. The seven-foot center was coming off a season at Arizona averaging a double-double with 20 points and 11.6 rebounds per game. At that time, the Suns already had a budding superstar in Devin Booker, and they thought that Ayton would be a good complement to the young guard.

The second pick of the draft went to the Sacramento Kings, a team which has the longest active streak in the NBA of not making it to the playoffs. With their pick, the Kings selected

Marvin Bagley, a center from Duke. Unlike Ayton, Bagley is a more versatile big man who had a more polished offensive game that extended beyond post-ups. While Ayton was a more dominant big man, the Kings believed that Bagley had what it took to turn the team around and hopefully put the franchise back in the running for a playoff spot.

The third pick of the draft went to the Atlanta Hawks. However, it was reported that the Atlanta Hawks and the Dallas Mavericks had negotiated that they would be exchanging picks for the first round. So, even though the Atlanta Hawks technically drafted Luka Doncic, the Slovenian guard would end up with the Dallas Mavericks by the end of the night. Consequently, the Dallas Mavericks drafted guard Trae Young on behalf of the Hawks. Interestingly enough, Young and Doncic would be the two best performers of their draft class as they would end up vying for the top two spots of Rookie of the Year by the end of the season.

This was a critical time for the Mavericks as their long-time superstar Dirk Nowitzki, who served as the face of the franchise for two decades, was facing retirement. By drafting Luka, they put themselves in the position of building the next phase of the franchise around the talents of the EuroLeague MVP.

In hindsight, many experts and pundits agree that Luka should have gone as the first overall pick during the draft. Aside from the fact that he would end up outperforming any of the other players in his class, he also had the advantage of already proving himself against professionals in the EuroLeague.

Chapter 4: Career Highlights and Achievements

Luka Doncic has only played a total of four seasons in the NBA so far, with two of them being shortened due to the COVID-19 pandemic. Despite this, Luka has managed to cement his status as one of the most amazing and entertaining players in the world. In this chapter, we are going to take a year-by-year run of Luka's career so far in the NBA. From this, we can analyze the momentum that he has been able to build and sustain since entering the league as a 19-year-old. Then, we can start to speculate on what the rest of his career could possibly look like.

Year One: The Boy Wonder

By getting drafted into the league after already having experienced playing professionally overseas, Doncic was at somewhat of an advantage over the rest of the players in his draft class. Regardless, getting drafted to the NBA and actually fulfilling one's expectations are two very different things. Despite not getting drafted first overall, the expectations were high for Doncic, considering everything that he had accomplished in the EuroLeague at such a young age. But many were still skeptical of his abilities because of the fact that he hadn't yet proved himself on American soil.

Doncic was riding the momentum of having won a EuroLeague MVP and the EuroLeague Final Four MVP while also leading his Real Madrid team to the 2018 championship. And the Dallas Mavericks obviously saw something special in him by choosing to trade for him in the draft for another exciting young player in Trae Young. The situation in Dallas was almost too perfect for Doncic to pass up. Another European legend who many regard to be the greatest European basketball player of all time, Dirk Nowitzki had hinted that the 2018-2019 season would be his last. That meant that Doncic would have the privilege and opportunity to play his rookie year together with perhaps the best import to have ever graced an NBA floor.

Dirk was no stranger to being doubted by people before eventually proving himself to be the legend that he was. When he first got to the NBA, the idea of an international superstar actually being among the best players in the league was relatively unheard of. It was very rare for international players to make a successful jump to the NBA and classify themselves along the elite. And even though it took a while, Dirk managed to do just that. He managed to lead the Mavericks to the Finals twice, both in 2006 and 2011, with the latter being a successful campaign and the franchise's first championship. He also racked up an MVP award in 2007 that only added to his long list of accolades.

Doncic's first year with the Mavericks was almost like a ceremonial passing of the torch from one superstar to another.

Even though Dirk still showed some occasional signs of brilliance, he was undoubtedly far from his peak form. The Mavericks knew that they needed to find a new superstar to fill Dirk's shoes and they turned to Luka, who was more than ready for the task. While many thought that it would probably take some time for Luka to adjust to the pace of the NBA game, the European superstar didn't waste any time getting to work. He didn't even wait for the official season to start before sending shockwaves throughout the NBA world.

Preseason games aren't usually taken all that seriously by fans and the media. It's usually just a series of games that are designed to help players get loose and to help coaches experiment with a few different sets and plays before the start of the actual season. However, it appears that Luka Doncic didn't get the memo. In this particular case, the Dallas Mavericks were scheduled to take on the Beijing Ducks from the Chinese Basketball Association. While not too many people were interested in watching the Mavericks take on a relatively unknown pro-team from the other side of the world, many were eager to see how Doncic would fare in his debut with the team.

Barely two minutes into the start of the game, with the score at 5-3 in favor of the Mavericks, a Chinese basketball player launched a potential game-tying midrange jumper. The ball hit the rim just at the right velocity and direction so that it bounced Doncic's way, giving him his first touch of the ball in the NBA.

He immediately pushed the ball up the floor with heavy pressure from his Chinese opponents. By the time he had gotten to the paint, three Beijing Ducks were surrounding him and looking to contest his shot. Doncic had the option of dropping the ball off to a trailing teammate or kicking it back to an open Mavericks player at the three-point line. But *Cool-Hand Luka* was determined to get his first bucket in the NBA right away. After surveying the paint, Luka gathered himself and jumped up while simultaneously allowing a Beijing Duck to fly by him before making the layup. And that marked his first basket on an NBA floor.

The Mavericks would go on to blow out the Beijing Ducks, with Doncic finishing with a stat line of 16 points, 6 rebounds, 3 blocks, and 2 assists in his preseason debut. He also shot 3 out of 4 from three that game and was a marvel to behold during his time on the court. And even though Doncic shone in that game, many were still skeptical about how he would fare against actual NBA teams made up of real NBA superstars. That's why the first actual game of the regular season for the Dallas Mavericks would be a big one for Doncic and for the sports world itself.

On October 17, 2018, in the opening week of the NBA season, the Dallas Mavericks were scheduled to face off against the Phoenix Suns. This was a notable matchup because the Suns were also eager to field the number-one overall pick of that year's draft, DeAndre Ayton. Many at that time still felt that Luka had been the most logical choice for the number-one pick of the draft, given his success in the EuroLeague at such a young age while playing against seasoned veterans. But Ayton had also held his own with his successful college stint to go along with this limitless potential and formidable size. And in the very first possession of the game, Luka was eager to show the world that he wasn't afraid of Ayton and that he was going to take the game into his own hands.

In their first possession of the game, Doncic received a high screen from his teammate DeAndre Jordan who was subsequently being guarded by DeAndre Ayton. The screen forced a switch that saw Ayton now covering Luka, who was barreling himself to the bucket. Luka gathered the ball and leapt up into the air as if to challenge Ayton at the rim with a layup. Ayton was forced to commit to defending Luka, which allowed Jordan to slip toward the rim undefended. Doncic then dropped the ball off to DeAndre for an uncontested slam— a simple pick-and-roll play to the eyes of many, but a statement from Doncic saying that he wasn't afraid of taking control of the game even if he was just a rookie.

The Suns would later go on to win that game 121-100 behind the heroics of Devin Booker, and Doncic himself had a relatively underwhelming debut with a stat line of 10 points, 8 rebounds, and 4 assists. But what the stat line doesn't show was the savvy and level of ball control that Luka displayed all throughout the game. While it wasn't necessarily a mind-blowing performance from Doncic, he would get a shot at really showcasing his prowess as a basketball player just a month later.

On November 17, 2018, the Dallas Mavericks would have their hands full as they faced off against the two-time defending champion Golden State Warriors. Granted, Draymond Green and Stephen Curry were sitting the game out with injuries. But the Warriors still had a formidable squad led by two-time Finals MVP Kevin Durant and sharpshooter Klay Thompson.

Doncic was all smiles during the pre-game shootaround, showing no visible signs of nerves or anxiety. And this confidence carried over into the actual game as well. All throughout the game, Luka cemented his mark on the game with a series of flashy passes, tough shots, and hard rebounds. The underdog Mavericks squad fought tooth and nail to try to keep pace with the defending champs. Harrison Barnes also chipped in with a good performance, contributing 23 points for the game. The two teams exchanged haymakers with one another until the very end.

With just a little over a minute left in regulation, the Mavericks were down by one with the score at 108-107. Doncic had the ball at the top of the key and forced a switch on a pick-and-roll play. He now had Jonas Jerebko on him, who was significantly slower and less athletic than Doncic. The young star took advantage of this mismatch and used a series of flashy dribbles to get into the paint before nailing a soft floater over the outstretched arms of

Jerebko, giving the Mavericks the lead. That floater would eventually serve as the final nail in the Warriors' coffin as they would never recover the lead after that. The Luka-led Mavericks eventually toppled the defending champions 112-109. This game caused NBA spectators, media members, and players to start paying closer attention to Luka and the Mavericks.

Even though the Mavericks never really solidified themselves as serious contenders during that year, with a roster full of inexperienced younglings and aging veterans, Luka served as the lone shining light for that team's season. He would go on to have one of the most dominant rookie campaigns in recent memory. On January 27th and February 2nd, Luka would have games against the eventual champion Toronto Raptors and Cleveland Cavaliers respectively. During these two games, he scored 35 points each, which marked his season high.

But there was something even more special about that Raptors game that not a lot of people realize. Luka Doncic actually made NBA history by being the first teenager to ever record a 30-point triple-double performance, making him the youngest player to ever achieve such an accolade. The record was previously held by Lonzo Ball and Lebron James, who were both 20 years old when they achieved the feat. What's even more impressive about that Raptors game was that he was going up against the team that would eventually win it all that year. This was a team that was composed of a roster of savvy defenders including Kawhi

Leonard, Kyle Lowry, Pascal Siakam, Danny Green, and Serge Ibaka. Despite the defensive prowess of that Raptor team under the leadership of head coach Nick Nurse, all of them had a problem defending against a 19-year-old Slovenian kid in his first year in the league. The Raptors would eventually win the game 123-120, but the entire team was put on notice by Luka and his talents.

Doncic would finish the night with 35 points, 12 rebounds, and 10 assists, which was arguably his best game of the season. More than just the stats that he was able to accumulate, Doncic showed immense talent with the way that he methodically took control of the game. He displayed a vast array of decisive passes that led to easy baskets for his teammates. He also showed off his creativity with his dribble penetration as he found various angles to attack the hoop from. Doncic also displayed his soft shooting touch with a few jumpers from long range to highlight his versatility as a scoring machine.

Doncic's efforts notched him his second of 8 triple-doubles that he would eventually get during that year. A triple-double is a statistical indicator that is often used to measure a player's overall impact on the game in various aspects. Doncic's 8 triple-doubles during his rookie year would also historically place him as third all-time in the list of most triple-doubles ever by a player during their rookie season. He sits just behind Ben Simmons and Oscar Robertson, who notched 12 and 26 triple-doubles during their rookie years. It's also worth noting that Doncic sits ahead of all-time great Magic Johnson on that list.

Despite his fantastic season, the Mavericks would end up with a losing record of 33-49, rendering them ineligible for the playoffs. However, it wasn't all bad at the end of the season, as Luka Doncic edged out Trae Young for the coveted Rookie of the Year award. Ironically enough, the Hawks had traded Doncic at the draft in favor of Young. Doncic would eventually round the year out with a stat line of 21.2 points, 7.8 rebounds, and 6 assists per game. Young averaged 19.1 points, 8.1 assists, and 3.7 assists while leading the Hawks to a 29-53 record on the year. Doncic garnered a landslide victory in voting as he managed to get 98 out of a possible 100 first-place votes for the award to go along with two second-place votes. Luka also earned a spot as a member of the 2018-2019 All-Rookie First Team.

Even though the numbers suggest that Doncic was by far and away the lock-in favorite for the award, Young's performance in the latter parts of the season really gave Luka a run for his money. Even NBA superstar Donovan Mitchell posted a Tweet on March 24th of that year declaring Trae Young as his pick for the best rookie that season after the Hawks outdueled a loaded Philly squad behind Trae's 32 points. Another NBA star Kyle Kuzma retweeted Mitchell's take and seconded his vote for Young. A former rookie of the year himself, Blake Griffin, retweeted Kuzma's take and clamored for Young to win the award as well.

There was a late-season surge on the part of Young and his performance as a talented individual. But Doncic's consistent play over the course of the entire season and his accumulated body of work made it difficult for anyone to argue against his case for the coveted award. Many of the league's greatest players of all time have won this award and it tends to be a good indicator of what kind of career a young NBA player is going to have. Whatever the case, Doncic will go down as having one of the most dominant rookie seasons that an NBA player has ever had.

Year Two: Sophomore Stardom (The Bubble Year)

Sophomore slumps happen way too frequently in the NBA. It happens a lot with rookies who showcase a tremendous amount of talent during their first year only to have their light eventually fade out during the second. Also, it's worth noting that many players in a typical draft class can sometimes take years before they fully adjust to the pace and style of play in the NBA. That's why a lot of players who perform relatively poorly during their first years still end up becoming all-star players three or four years down the line. With the historic rookie season that he had, there was so much pressure on Luka to sustain his run and dominance in the NBA with a stellar sophomore season. And with expectations that high, it was definitely an uphill battle for the young Mavericks star.

Luka didn't waste any time putting these speculations to bed. On October 25th, the Mavs were scheduled to face off against a young and talented Pelicans squad. Despite not being the most athletic player in the league, Luka still has one of the most formidable physiques in the NBA, and he isn't afraid of showcasing his strength when facing off against guards who are usually much smaller than he is. This time, he would be facing off against one of the bigger and stronger defensive point guards of the league in Lonzo Ball. And while Ball's size and strength certainly gave Luka a few problems throughout the game, the European star still managed to showcase the full range of his abilities in a 123-116 victory over the Pelicans.

With just two minutes left in the game, the Mavericks were up by two and Luka had the ball in his hands. After a series of flashy escape dribbles on the wing, Luka blew by his defenders, only to be greeted by two more Pelican big men in the paint. Doncic responded by throwing up a soft floater above their outstretched arms and managed to make the basket, extending their lead to 4. After getting a defensive stop and regaining possession of the ball, Doncic called for a screen just as he crossed half-court with the ball in his hands. He made an effort to drive toward the basket, only to be cut off by the rolling big man. Using his momentum against him, Doncic shifted directions and stepped back to the three-point line to gain some separation between himself and his defender. He then launched a three-point bomb that went in off the glass, which essentially iced the game for the Mavs. Doncic finished with 25 points, 10 rebounds, and 10 assists, notching his first of many triple-doubles for the year.

During the first quarter of the season, it really looked like Doncic didn't skip a beat in terms of his development as a budding talent in the league. Throughout the history of the NBA, there have only been three players to average at least 25 points at the age of 20. At this age, Kevin Durant was averaging 25.3 points per game and LeBron James was averaging 27.2 points per game. During the first quarter of his sophomore year as a 20-year-old, Luka Doncic was averaging 30 points per game. By the time December was rolling around, Luka was merely a rebound and an assist shy of averaging a triple double. He was also ranked third in the league in scoring and second in assists. By the looks of it, Luka wasn't going to have a sophomore slump at all. In fact, it looked like he was headed for sophomore stardom.

On November 9th, the Mavericks faced off against their Texan rival San Antonio Spurs. Doncic would finish the night with a then-career-high 42 points to go along with 12 assists and 11 rebounds. The Mavericks needed all that they could get from the young superstar as they grinded out a 117-110 win against the Popovich-led Spurs. It was Doncic's go-ahead three-pointer with just 26.5 seconds left in the fourth that eventually put the game away and sealed the win for the Mavs. For his efforts, Luka earned another triple-double, which would serve as his 6th of the year and the 14th of his career. Luka also became the only player together with Lebron James to score a 40-point triple-double as a 20-year-old.

On December 7th of that year, Luka cemented his name in the history books once more. In a game against the New Orleans Pelicans, Luka was absolutely balling out. The entire Mavericks team was firing on all fronts, so much so that Luka wasn't even called in to play for the entire fourth quarter. Despite sitting out the last quarter, Luka still finished with 26 points, 9 rebounds, and 6 assists. He managed to accumulate these stats in just 26 minutes of play. While this stat line isn't necessarily all that impressive, it did signify an important milestone in Luka's career that would put him in the record books. It was his 18th straight game with at least 20 points, 5 rebounds, and 5 assists. This put him at a tie with Michael Jordan, who many regard to be the greatest basketball player of all time. Luka would later go on to extend that streak to 20 total games. Unfortunately, the streak would come to an end on December 15 after Luka Doncic had to leave the game early in a matchup against Miami due to an ankle injury that would sideline him for 12 days. He finished the game with just two points and one rebound in a minute of play.

The NBA was marred with tragedy throughout 2020. At the start of the year, the former NBA commissioner David Stern passed away as the result of a brain hemorrhage. Just a few weeks after that, NBA legend Kobe Bryant died in a tragic helicopter crash that put the whole world into a state of mourning. This was also the year that would eventually come to be known as the *bubble year*, wherein the NBA conducted a portion of the season in a quarantined bubble within Disney World in Florida.

As the year started, however, things still continued to look bright for Luka and the rise of his stardom. On January 4th, Luka notched his tenth triple-double of the season with a massive stat line of 39 points, 12 rebounds, and 10 assists in a close loss to the Charlotte Hornets. Luka went on a run of great games that grabbed the attention of fellow players, coaches, and fans from around the world. His impressive year so far would earn him a starting spot at the 2020 All-Star Game. Despite missing out on an invitation in the year prior, many fans still felt like he deserved a slot on the team during his rookie season. As a result of his selection in 2020, Doncic became the youngest European player to start in the All-Star game. And in 18 minutes of action, Luka was able to put up 8 points and 4 assists in a game that went down to the wire.

Luka was having a magical year and he was on pace to carry the Mavericks all the way to playoff contention after not making it the previous year. However, in March of that year, the NBA had decided to temporarily postpone games as a result of the rising spread of the COVID-19 virus. It was an unprecedented move on the part of the NBA in response to a once-in-a-lifetime occurrence. Several NBA players had contracted the virus and the entire season was put on hold while the league officials scrambled to figure out a way to safely officiate the remaining games of the year. After many months of inactivity, the league introduced a concept that had never been done by any sports league in history: a bubble. The NBA bubble was designed to be an enclosed space that housed the entirety of the league's team players, trainers, coaches, management, and staff. This accounted for hundreds of NBA personnel in a single place without any physical contact to the outside world for around three months or so.

With the way that the bubble was structured, the NBA enlisted the assistance of Disney World in Orlando. The theme park served as a viable place for a bubble that could be able to function as a miniaturized city for athletes. The park was already fitted with hotels, kitchens, fitness gyms, and basketball courts where the games could be held. Aside from having all of the teams present for the bubble, the NBA only invited 22 teams that were still eligible for playoff contention. And it just so happened that Luka's Mavericks were one of the teams.

The conditions inside the bubble were deemed infamous by players, coaches, and team staff alike. Every day, all of the people within the bubble were subjected to COVID-19 testing and isolation protocols. Aside from that, players were not allowed to exit and enter the bubble as they pleased. The NBA commissioned food service providers to offer the teams various catering options for their meals. This lack of mobility and freedom was a new challenge for many NBA players who were used to travelling for their games. In fact, many NBA players deemed the concept of the bubble so absurd that they decided to opt out of participating. Before the season resumed in the bubble, the Dallas Mavericks were positioned as the seventh team in the west with a 40-27 record.

Despite the unfamiliar conditions brought forth by playing in the bubble, Luka still displayed the brilliance that he had been showcasing consistently all year. On August 8th, 2020, Luka had an incredible stat line against one of the premiere teams of the east, the Milwaukee Bucks. Doncic got things going early in the game with a series of shake-and-bake moves to fly by Wesley Matthews as he dove to the rim for an uncontested layup. Little did the Bucks know that they would be in for a serious challenge from the young Slovenian. The Bucks had already clinched the number-one spot in the east and the Mavericks were still jockeying for better position in the west. Luka wanted to send a message to the league-leading Bucks with a stellar performance that night.

As the game wore on, the Mavericks were able to keep pace with a Bucks squad that had dominated the NBA all year with a record of 55-14. Luka was dishing the ball to teammates left and right for wide-open jumpers and easy layups. He dominated the ball himself with a series of flashy drives to the hoop and his patented step back jumpers. Both teams traded blows back and forth until there were just 21 seconds left in regulation with the Mavs down by two. Luka had been fouled on his way to the basket and was now tasked with having to drain two clutch free throws in order to keep the Mavs alive. Cool Hand Luka had already amassed 32 points, 15 assists, and 11 rebounds at that point, netting him another triple-double for the year. Doncic swished both free throws and put the game into overtime.

With just a minute and 15 seconds left on the clock and the Mavs up by two with possession of the ball, Luka called for a give-and-go ball screen with Maxi Kleber. Doncic put pressure on the defense by driving hard toward the basket with Kleber trailing just beside him. Luka successfully commanded the attention of Giannis Antetokounmpo, the eventual league MVP for that year and the Bucks' best defender. Luka then swiftly made the highlight of the night with a between-the-legs bounce pass to the trailing Kleber, who finished strong at the rim with an and-1 play. The Bucks battled hard and managed to reduce the Mavs' lead down to three with 30 seconds left in overtime. On the next possession, Luka decided to take the game into his own hands and barreled toward the rim under heavy pressure from his defender Eric Bledsoe. As Doncic approached the paint, Giannis went over to him to help challenge the shot, but it wasn't enough. Doncic sank a soft floater over the outstretched arm of

Antetokounmpo, which would seal the victory for the Mavs. Doncic finished the night with 36 points, 19 assists, and 14 rebounds in 42 minutes of play. This game was historic for two reasons. First, it would serve as Luka's then career-high for assists in a game with 19. Aside from that, his performance would give him his 17th triple-double of the season, thereby clinching his status as the youngest player to ever lead the NBA in triple-doubles in a season.

In the eight games that he played to finish off the NBA season as a part of their "Seeding Games" in the bubble, Luka averaged 30 points, 10.1 rebounds, and 9.7 assists, along with a handful of clutch moments and heavy-hitting performances. He would later be named to the NBA's All-Seeding Games First Team. He would also be named to the All-NBA First Team that year. This made him the only player since Tim Duncan to be selected to the All-NBA First Team in their first or second season. And despite his MVP-caliber numbers, it was Giannis Antetokounmpo who would eventually win the most coveted individual award of that year. This wasn't a big surprise to many, as Giannis led his team to getting the best record in the NBA during the regular season. Doncic finished fourth overall in voting for MVP and he became the second-youngest player in history to be part of the top five of the MVP voting. Ironically enough, despite winning Rookie of the Year in the previous year, Luka still finished in the top three of voting for the NBA's Most Improved Player Award.

Aside from his individual accolades, this would also be the first year that the Mavericks would make the playoffs under Luka's leadership. And in his playoff debut, Luka certainly didn't disappoint. The Mavericks were positioned to face off against an overpowered Los Angeles Clippers squad who had two of the leagues' best defenders and two-way players in Paul George and Kawhi Leonard. Of course, Luka was up to the challenge and was eager to show off in his first ever NBA playoff game. The young star finished the game with 42 points and again set another NBA record as the most points ever scored by an NBA player in their playoff debut. However, the Clippers still proved to be too much for the Mavs as they dealt the Luka-led squad a 118-110 loss. However, just a few days later, Luka would get his revenge on the Clippers by having what may have been the best game of his career up to that point.

The Clippers were up in the series 2-1 and Dallas knew that they needed to secure a win in order to stay competitive in the series. Teams that go down 3-1 in a playoff series in the NBA have less than a 0.05% chance of coming back to win. The game started off as a sloppy slugfest with both teams struggling to gain any kind of offensive momentum. Both teams traded blows with one another for all four quarters with Paul George, Lou Williams, and Kawhi Leonard doing a lot of the heavy lifting for the Clippers. Not to be outdone, Doncic did everything he could to keep the Mavs in the game with a combination of fadeaway shots, scoop layups, and pinpoint passes to get his teammates open shots.

Eventually, the score would remain tied at the end of regulation, thereby forcing overtime.

The slugfest continued into the overtime period with both teams trading haymakers with one another. Aside from the usual stars coming out to play, many of the role players stepped up to keep things competitive. With just 25 seconds left in overtime and the score tied at 130 all, Luka Doncic had the ball at the top of the key with a smaller Reggie Jackson defending him. After a couple of hesitation dribbles, Luka crossed the ball over to his left side as he made his way toward the free throw line, only to spin back toward the other side at the lest second. Jackson stayed with him all throughout the possession, but Doncic's footwork gave him enough space to lay the ball up and in through the net.

On the next possession, the Clippers' Kawhi Leonard had the ball on the right wing. Leonard had previously hit an iconic game-winning shot in the previous playoffs against the Philadelphia 76ers that would allow his Toronto Raptors team to eventually win the NBA championship. So, many of the Mavs defenders had their eyes on Leonard all throughout the possession. After a slight dribble hesitation, he made his move toward the ring in the middle of the floor. As several Mavs defenders collapsed into the paint to help, Leonard dished the ball over to a wide-open Marcus Morris, who was standing in the corner. Morris drained the open three-pointer to put the Clippers up by one with just nine seconds left on the clock.

The Mavs fumbled their next possession, but they still retained possession of the ball with 3.7 seconds left in overtime. With so little time remaining, the Mavs needed to draw up a quick play that would allow them to get a bucket before the time expired. Dorian Finney-Smith was tasked with throwing the ball inbounds to Luka Doncic, who had just received a flare screen from Maxi Kleber. Doncic was defended by Reggie Jackson, who struggled to keep up with Luka's dribble moves. The Slovenian talent made for a move toward the center of the floor before crossing the ball over back to the left side for a step back three-pointer from way behind the arc. The ball swooshed right through the net as the buzzer sounded, sealing the win for the Mavs, who had tied the series at two games apiece with the higher-seeded Clippers. In that game, Doncic garnered 43 points, 17 rebounds, and 13 assists. With that, he became the youngest player in NBA history to get a 40-point triple-double. He also became just the second player to record at least 43 points, 17 rebounds, and 13 assists since Wilt Chamberlain did it back in the 60s.

The Mavs would eventually be eliminated by the Clippers in six games, resulting in a first-round exit for Doncic in his first-ever playoffs. But at that point, Doncic had sent the league a message. Despite his age and relative inexperience, he was a force to be reckoned with in the coming seasons.

Year Three: The Division Title

After breaking the Mavs' three-year slump of missing the postseason while solidifying himself as an MVP-caliber player, the expectations were high for Luka Doncic heading into year three of his career. Of course, this wasn't unfamiliar territory for Doncic. The expectations were already high for him during his sophomore year, and he surpassed everyone's expectations with flying colors. Would he be able to finally clinch the most coveted individual player accomplishment in the NBA by being voted MVP? After successfully carrying the Mavs into the playoffs, would he be able to lead them past the first round? These were just some of the questions that fans, critics, and spectators were asking surrounding Doncic's third year in the league.

The season started off with a grim outlook as the Mavs team just didn't look ready for the start of the season. Luka was still putting up spectacular numbers, but they weren't quite the same kinds of performances that he had given the year before. At one point, in early February, the Mavericks had a record of 9-14. They were performing so poorly that there were huge doubts that they would make it back to the playoffs again. Things looked especially bad after they lost six straight games to end the month of January. But that losing streak was the worst that the Mavericks would endure for the rest of the regular season.

After February 1st, the Mavericks would never lose more than two consecutive games for the rest of the season's schedule. In a stretch from March to April, the Mavericks went on a season-high five-game win streak that saw their record improve to 28-21. The Mavericks, a team that was in jeopardy of missing out on the playoffs for the fourth time in five years, finished the regular season off with a record of 42-30. This was good enough for them to secure the fifth seed in the Western Conference playoff picture and a division title as well. This was the first time that the Mavs would win a division title since 2010 when German basketball legend Dirk Nowitzki was at the helm.

Along the way, Luka again cemented his name in the league's record books with a number of historical achievements and milestones. In a game against the Golden State Warriors, Luka carried the Mavericks to a win behind a heroic 42-point effort along with 11 assists and 7 rebounds. Just a few days after that, Doncic would secure his then career-high of 46 points paired with 12 assists and 8 rebounds to win a close game against the New Orleans Pelicans. A few weeks after that, Doncic put on a passing clinic in a game against the Washington Wizards. The superstar managed to finish the game with 31 points and 12 rebounds. But the most impressive stat of the night was his career-high 20 assists. Luka made the game look so easy as he set his teammates up for easy shots all night long to help get them in the game. And after winning by just three points, it turns out that the Mavs needed everything that they could get from Luka that night. His performance allowed him to become just the fourth player in NBA history to score at least 30 points, 10 rebounds, and 20 assists. The other three players to have such a distinction are Magic Johnson, Oscar Robertson, and Russell Westbrook.

Less than a week after his historic game against the Pelicans, the Mavs would face off against the underperforming Cleveland Cavaliers in what was, on paper, just another regular season matchup. The Mavs got off to a good start and it looked like they were looking to make quick and easy work of the Cavs en route to their 39th win of the season. Four minutes into the start of the game, Luka got the ball deep in the paint and challenged Cleveland's premiere shot blocker Jared Allen for a shot. The ball bounced off of the rim right back into Luka's hand. Without skipping a beat, Luka jumped back up to attempt another shot and was fouled in the process.

As Doncic trudged toward the line for two shots, he was just two points away from reaching 5,000 total points for his career. Luka nonchalantly sank both free throws to accomplish the milestone. This made him the fastest Mavericks player in history to achieve such a feat. Aside from that, he became the fourth-youngest player in league history to net 5,000 total career points behind LeBron James, Kevin Durant, and Carmelo Anthony. What makes this milestone even more impressive for Luka was the fact that his first seasons were shortened due to complications brought about by the COVID-19 pandemic. That career milestone served as the icing on the cake for a productive Mavs season that looked like it was already doomed early in the year.

But the year wasn't over, and Luka knew that the world was expecting him and his team to make waves in the playoffs after what they had accomplished the year before. Unfortunately, as fate would have it, the Mavericks were slated to take on the Los Angeles Clippers once more. This was the same team that forced the Mavericks out of the playoffs in the first round in the previous year, and many questioned whether Luka and his team had what it took to overcome their western conference foes. In fact, most of the world thought that the Mavs would be able to put up a fight, but would eventually just bow out to the Clippers, just like the previous year.

The first game of the series started off in favor of the Mavericks as the young team shot out to a quick 9-2 lead in the first three minutes of the first quarter. Doncic was aggressive right at the start of the game as he looked to dominate the Clippers' premiere perimeter defender, Patrick Beverley. Even though Beverley had amassed a solid reputation as being a dependable defender in the league, he was visibly struggling against a much bigger and stronger Doncic. Luka easily overpowered Beverley in multiple plays toward the hoop as he found easy baskets close to the rim. The game was a bit of a slugfest with both teams exchanging runs to keep things close. Kawhi Leonard took control of the game on the Clippers' end as he showcased his playoff experience and formidable skill. But Luka proved that he could hold his own against this elite Clipper team the same way that he was able to in the previous year. With 35 seconds left in the first half, Doncic saw an opportunity to increase the Mavs' 57-53 lead going into halftime. He had the ball at the top of the key with a much slower Marcus Morris defending him. The all-star guard called for a pick from his teammate Dorian Finney-Smith, which put Morris out of position on defense. Doncic then proceeded to sidestep his way to an open three-pointer that put the Mavs up 60-53 going into halftime. Suddenly, the underdog Mavericks were just two quarters away from taking the first game of the series.

The Clippers rallied back early in the second half to keep the game close, but Doncic continued to drain a barrage of difficult shots against the Clippers. It took the effort of both Paul George and Kawhi Leonard to try to keep pace with Doncic and the Mavs. But the young Mavs team was riding on their own momentum as they eventually surged toward a game-one victory against the Clippers. Doncic finished the night with 31 points, 10 rebounds, and 11 assists. This made him the first-ever player in league history to have had three triple-doubles within their first seven games in the playoffs for their career. He also achieved another notable milestone as the youngest player to have ever recorded a triple-double while on the road in the playoffs. This was a record that was previously held by the NBA's all-time leading scorer Kareem Abdul-Jabbar.

This scrappy Mavs team rallied behind their leader as they went on to win the second game of the series as well. Suddenly, it started to look like the Clippers were on the ropes and were in jeopardy of being on the losing end of an upset to the Mavs. After all, teams that go up 2-0 in a series have historically shown to have more than a 90% chance of winning the matchup. However, the playoff experience of the Clippers proved to be very important, as they were able to rally back from being down 2-0 to tie the series and eventually force a do-or-die seventh game against Doncic and the Mavs. This would also end up being Doncic's first Game 7 in his career and many were eager to see how the young star would fare.

There was a palpable energy in the air as neither team wanted their seasons to be cut short. Game 7s in the NBA are always a big deal, especially when it involves two rival teams who have had a substantial history in facing off with one another. While the nerves were high for everyone involved, Doncic conducted himself like an absolute veteran in the very first play of the game. After receiving the ball from the tip-off, Doncic passed the ball to his teammate Boban Marjanovic before positioning himself down in the high post. Doncic had a smaller Reggie Jackson guarding him, and he took his time with his back to the basket while surveying the floor for his possible options. Most superstars are eager to get the first score during games like these just to break the ice and get rid of the nerves. But Doncic acted as coolly and calmly as possible as he waited for an opportunity to arise in the form of his teammate Tim Hardaway Jr. running uncontested to the rim. Doncic promptly bulleted a pass toward Hardaway, who then proceeded to lay the ball in for the first basket of the game.

Not to be outdone, two-time Finals MVP Kawhi Leonard then proceeded to drain a fadeaway midrange jumper in their first possession to tie the game at two points apiece. The rest of the game carried on similarly to how the matchups between these two teams had previously gone. The stars were consistently controlling the pace of the game while putting up their regular numbers. Paul George and Kawhi Leonard took turns in carrying the scoring load for the Clippers. But the supporting cast of Reggie Jackson and Marcus Morris also made some contributions of their own. The Mavericks countered with a huge frontline of Boban Marjanovic and Kristaps Porzingis to help make it a little more difficult for the Clippers to finish down low. On the other end of the floor, Luka unleashed a full arsenal of step back threes and drives to the rim in order to create scoring opportunities for himself and his teammates. By the end of the first quarter, things were looking good for the Mavericks as they led the Clippers 38-35. Doncic accounted for half of his team's first quarter points with 19 of his own. It was obvious that, even though both teams had faced one another numerous times over the past two years, the Clippers still had no answer for Doncic's offensive prowess.

With Luka resting on the bench to start off the second quarter, the Clippers seized the opportunity to mount a run of their own with their deep roster of bench players. Mavericks head coach Rick Carlisle could see that the Mavs were struggling to generate any momentum on their own without Doncic on the floor. Carlisle didn't wait too long before subbing Doncic back in after just a couple minutes of rest. The Clippers had managed to grow their lead to 46-40 before Doncic answered back with a fadeaway jumper that cut the lead back to four with seven minutes left in the quarter. Both the Clippers and Mavericks exchanged buckets with one another as the Los Angeles squad clung on to a semi-comfortable lead for a huge stretch of the second quarter. But with less than five minutes left in the quarter, Doncic quite literally took the ball into his own hands and drove past three Clippers defenders to finish strong at the rim as he was fouled in the process. Luka would then go on to sink the and-1, giving him his 26th point of the game and cutting the Clippers lead down to two with more than four minutes to go in the half. The Clippers would go on a mini-run of their own to extend the lead back to seven. Doncic responded by draining his trademark step back three that so many players have come to fear in the NBA. The Mavs superstar would finish the half with 29 points, but it wouldn't be enough as the Clippers would go into halftime with a 70-62 lead.

At the start of the third quarter, the Mavericks hit the floor with a vengeance as they slowly chipped away at the Clippers lead and eventually closed the gap within five minutes of play. With a little more than seven minutes left in the quarter and the game tied, Doncic brought the ball up the court and called for a screen from Dorian Finney-Smith, who then proceeded to split the screen and popped out to the three-point line for an open shot courtesy of a Doncic assist. This put the Mavs up by three and would give them their first lead since the start of the second quarter. On their next possession, Porzingis would bank a contested layup off the board to give the Mavs their largest lead of the game at five after being down eight at the half.

With their season on the line, the Clippers would then go on a formidable run of their own. With just a little under a minute left in the game, Clippers backup guard Luke Kinnard sank a corner three that would cap off a 21-2 run by the Clippers and put them back up by 14 points. Doncic then put a stop to the bleeding by executing a nifty euro step past three Clippers defenders on the way to point-blank bucket at the rim. On the next possession, Kinnard would respond with another three-pointer to extend the Clippers' lead to 15 going into the final quarter of the game.

Unfortunately for the Mavs, they would never be able to recover from the third-quarter Clipper run for the rest of the game. The Mavericks tried to battle back and showed some flashes of life. But the Clippers proved themselves to be far too overpowering for the young and inexperienced Mavericks squad. The Clippers would eventually edge out the Mavericks 126-111, thereby eliminating them in the first round of the playoffs for the second year in a row. They managed to do this behind the near triple-double effort of their superstar Kawhi Leonard, who finished the night with 28 points, 10 rebounds, and 9 assists. Luka ended up with a stat line and new playoff career-high of 46 points to go along with an astonishing 14 assists. But his heroic efforts were not enough to overcome the Clippers for a second straight year.

Despite the playoff disappointment, Luka still managed to bag his second selection to the All-NBA First Team. This made him the sixth player in history to be selected to the All-NBA First Team twice within their first three seasons.

Luka Doncic, The Olympian

One of the additional complications that was brought about by the COVID-19 pandemic was the postponement of the 2020 Tokyo Olympic games to 2021. And coming off a disappointing first round exit at the hands of the Los Angeles Clippers, Doncic didn't waste any time getting back to work. But this time, instead of suiting up for the Mavericks, Doncic donned a jersey with a different shade of blue for the Slovenian national team.

At 22 years old, Doncic was set to make his Olympic debut. But by the looks of the way that he performed in his first game on the global stage, one would have assumed that he was a seasoned veteran. Slovenia hasn't had the most decorated Olympic history. Since gaining its independence from Yugoslavia in 1991, Slovenia has failed to qualify for any Olympic games in the sport of basketball. This year marked the first time that the country would be participating in the Olympic basketball tournament in that entire span, and a young Luka Doncic would be captaining the squad.

In the opening game of the tournament, Slovenia was slated to face off against Argentina, a country with a rich basketball culture and one that has gained immense basketball success on the global stage. While Doncic may be one of the youngest athletes to participate in the Olympics, it certainly didn't show in the way that he outclassed a loaded Argentinian squad. Luka opened up his Olympic journey with a historic 48-point triple-double. His 48-point marker also ranked as third in the most points ever scored in a game in Olympic history.

The Slovenians performed very well at the start of their Olympic journey, winning all three of their group games. After that, they destroyed an experienced Germany team 94-70, which allowed them to advance to the semi-finals. The Slovenians were just one more win away from guaranteeing a medal finish at this year's Olympics. This is no small feat for a team that had never qualified for the Olympic games in the past. Unfortunately for the team, Luka Doncic suffered a wrist injury in the middle of the game after colliding with a plexiglass barrier. The injury essentially rendered Doncic ineffective as a scorer for the rest of the game. The Slovenian star didn't even attempt a single field goal for the entire quarter. In the last possession of regulation, Slovenia was down by just one point and had a chance to win the game at the buzzer. But France's Nicolas Batum, who was also a member of the Clippers team that tormented Doncic in the NBA, secured France's win with a topnotch defensive play. France eliminated Slovenia from contention and dealt Doncic his first loss on the international scene after 17 straight wins. Despite his injuries, Doncic still ended up with another triple-double stat line of 16 points, 18 assists, and 10 rebounds.

Doncic and the Slovenian team still had a chance at getting the bronze medal in a final match against an NBA-loaded Australian squad that featured stars like Patty Mills, Mattis Thybulle, Joe Ingles, Aaron Baynes, Dante Exum, and Matthew Dellavedova. The Slovenians had the odds stacked against them. The incredibly deep and talented Australian squad proved to be too much for the Slovenians. Doncic's wrist injury was still bothering him, and he ended up just shooting 7 out of 20 from the field. He ended up with 22 points, 8 rebounds, and 7 assists, which are respectable numbers, but not enough to overcome the Australians. This meant that Doncic would have to walk away from the 2020 Olympics without a medal to show for his efforts. Despite that, he still proved himself as an unstoppable force all throughout the tournament as he put the entire world on notice.

Year Four: Playoff Success

Even before the start of the NBA season, Luka Doncic made history once more by signing a five-year $207 million rookie extension with the Dallas Mavericks. This marked the largest rookie extension contract in NBA history. Going into this season, the major criticisms surrounding Doncic and his game were whether he would be able to elevate his defense to an elite level and whether he would be able to lead his team past the first round of the playoffs. In the previous two years, the Mavericks suffered heartbreaking defeats at the hands of the Los Angeles Clippers in the first round. While the expectations were high for Luka, not many people could envision him leading the team too deep into the playoffs.

There were a few shakeups concerning the team's personnel. On June 17, 2021, the team's head coach Rick Carlisle resigned from his head coaching job after 13 seasons. It's worth noting that Carlisle is the coach who is responsible for delivering the franchise's first and only NBA championship back in 2011 when the underdog Mavs upset the overpowered Miami Heat led by LeBron James. The team's long-time general manager Donnie Nelson also announced his departure from the team. It was reported that both Carlisle and Nelson's resignations were mutual decisions made by the team and the parties involved.

On June 28, Jason Kidd was hired to be the head coach of the team. Kidd's previous head coaching stints were with the

Brooklyn Nets from 2013 to 2014 and the Milwaukee Bucks from 2014-2018. Prior to being recruited by the Mavs for the head coaching position, Kidd was one of the assistant coaches on the Los Angeles Lakers squad that won the championship in the NBA bubble. Aside from having Kidd take over the team for his first year, the Mavs roster was composed of a very young squad. For most of the year, the Mavericks fielded a starting lineup of Luka Doncic, Jalen Brunson, Reggie Bullock, Dorian Finney-Smith, and Dwight Powell. They also heavily relied on the support of bench players Trey Burke, Spencer Dinwiddie, Josh Green, and Tim Hardaway Jr. Of those players mentioned, it was Burke, Bullock, and Hardaway Jr. who had the most NBA experience, having played in the league for eight years each. With the lack of playoff experience under a new system that was being led by Jason Kidd, very few people thought that the Mavericks would be able to make a serious dent in the playoffs.

To the surprise of many, the Mavericks would have its best regular season performance since its championship season in 2010-2011. The Mavericks finished second in their division in the southwest, failing to defend their division title. But they improved to fourth in the western conference with an astonishing record of 52 wins and 30 losses. The Mavericks never lost more than three consecutive games with Kidd at the helm. It took a while for the team to really meld together as a single unit. On January 1st, at the turn of the new year, the Mavericks had a 17-18 record. But after a 95-86 win against the Oklahoma City

Thunder on January 2nd, the team would go on to have one of the most magical stretches in the league for the whole of January. The Dallas Mavericks won 12 out of the 16 games that they played in January, the best record in the league for that span. By the end of the month, they had improved to a 29-22 record. Astonishingly enough, the Mavericks would continue to ride that momentum all the way to the end of the regular season. They would only go on to lose just 8 of the rest of their 31 games on the schedule. And that effort was good enough for the team to finish as the fourth seed in a competitive Western Conference.

Aside from the team success, Luka also notched a few milestones all throughout the season. In a win against the Philadelphia 76ers in early February, Luka logged 33 points, 13 rebounds, and 15 assists. This marked his 44th career triple-double, which moved him up to 10th on the list of all-time career triple-double leaders.

Just a few days after that, Luka secured a career-high 51 points against their rivals, the Los Angeles Clippers. Luka notched 28 of his 51 points in the first quarter of that game. He also ended up with 9 rebounds and 6 assists with 7 three-pointers. But Luka wasn't done with the Clippers just yet. The Mavs were scheduled to face the Clips in a back-to-back just a few days after, and Luka dropped 45 points, with 23 of them coming in the fourth. He also pulled down 15 rebounds and gave out 8 dimes in a losing effort to the Clippers. For his impressive stat line, Doncic was named the Western Conference Player of the Week.

Nearly a week after that, Luka almost eclipsed his new career high by getting 49 points in a 125-118 win over the New Orleans Pelicans. He paired his high scoring output with 15 rebounds and 8 assists to round out his complete game. Doncic carried on with his stellar play all throughout February on his way to becoming the first player in NBA history to average at least 30 points, 10 rebounds, and 8 assists per game while shooting at least 40% from three for an entire calendar month. He was also awarded the NBA Player of the Month award.

Unfortunately for the Mavericks, Doncic would suffer a minor calf strain on the last game of the regular season. This meant that he had to miss the first three games of the playoffs that year, in which they were penciled to take on the Utah Jazz. The Jazz had already shown consistency as being a perennial playoff team over the past few years. This was a Jazz team that was headed by the three-time Defensive Player of the Year Rudy Gobert and up-and-coming superstar Donavan Mitchell. Gobert was also a part of the France team that dealt Slovenia its heartbreak in the 2020 Tokyo Olympics. More than just seeking revenge on Gobert, Luka was eager to prove his doubters wrong and to lead his team past the first round.

Without their star player, the Mavericks had to defend their homecourt advantage against a mighty Jazz squad that came out focused and prepared. The Jazz would eventually go on to win the game 99-93. But many were surprised at how well the Mavericks fared against the Jazz despite not having Luka in the game. In fact, the Mavericks were performing so well that they ended up winning the next two games of the series to take a 2-1 lead over the Jazz. By then, Luka's injury had healed up and he was ready to lace his sneakers up for Game 4. Unfortunately, despite Luka's much-needed presence, the Mavericks fell to the Jazz in a heartbreaking 100-99 loss. The Jazz managed to tie the series at two games apiece with all games being decided by eight points or less. The fifth game of the series was a real shakeup as the Mavericks came out firing on all fronts en route to the first blowout of the series. The Mavs went up 3-2 by dealing the Jazz a devastating 102-77 loss. Now, Luka was just one game away from doing something he had never done before - leading his team past the first round. Game 6 was a back-and-forth affair as both teams traded blows with one another. The Jazz were looking to keep their season alive while the Mavs were eager to put their foes away for good.

The game would inevitably come down to the wire, with both teams tied at 94 with two minutes left in regulation. Bojan Bogdanovic had just nailed a clutch corner three to tie the game and the Mavericks needed to respond. After forcing the switch to get Rudy Gobert on him at the top of the key, Doncic used his speed advantage to blow by Gobert and get into the lane. As the Jazz defense collapsed to the inside in order to prevent a Doncic basket, the superstar playmaker quickly kicked the ball back out to a wide-open Jalen Brunson in the corner, who subsequently drained an uncontested three-pointer.

After trading missed shots in succeeding possessions, the Jazz's Donovan Mitchell quickly pushed the ball back up the floor before the Mavericks' defense could get set. He drove aggressively toward the rim and dropped off a pass to Rudy Gobert for a wide-open one-handed dunk to cut the Mavericks lead to one with 35 seconds left in regulation. The Mavs had one more chance to extend their lead as Luka drove hard to the rim and attempted a runner over the outstretched arms of the former Defensive Player of the Year Rudy Gobert. The Frenchman's height and length proved to be too much of a bother for Doncic, who missed the shot and gave the Jazz an opportunity to take the lead with the last possession of the game. With their series and season on the line, Jazz guard Mike Conley drove hard to the rim but was called for a travelling violation before the team could even attempt a shot. The Mavs' Jalen Brunson was intentionally fouled on the next play and drained one free throw to put the Mavericks up by two with four seconds left on the clock. The Jazz had one last attempt to keep their season alive with an inbounds play that allowed Jazz forward Bojan Bogdanovic to get a wide-open shot from three-point range. The ball clanked off the rim and this marked the first time since 2011 that the Mavericks would move on to the second round of the playoffs.

Even though Luka and the Mavs had so many reasons to celebrate, they needed to get their bearings together as they would now be facing the team with the best record during the regular season. The Phoenix Suns went 64-18 during the season behind a balanced attack that was spearheaded by sharpshooter Devin Booker, big man DeAndre Ayton, and veteran guard Chris Paul. The Suns also had the advantage of being coached by one of the best professionals in the NBA, Monty Williams. On paper, the Suns had everything that they needed to make short work of the young and inexperienced Mavericks squad that hadn't made it past the first round since 2011. The first two games of the series pretty much went the way that most people predicted. The Suns won both games, and many were already looking forward to a Western Conference matchup between the dominant Phoenix squad and a peaking Golden State Warriors team.

The Mavs tried their best to keep their season alive with an impressive effort in Game 3 that allowed them to secure a 103-94 win. In Game 4, the underdog Mavericks managed to make the Suns sweat just a little more by stealing another win at home. At this point, the series was tied at 2-2, and the Mavericks needed just two more wins to complete the upset against the Suns. But this Suns team had experienced their fair share of heartbreaks before and were not going to take this lying down. They came out with guns blazing in Game 5 as they blew the Mavs out early on the way to a 110-80 landslide win. The Mavericks were now back in familiar territory and had their backs against the wall. The younglings rose to the call and dominated the Suns in an easy 113-86 victory. Luka and the Mavs had forced a decisive Game 7 in a competitive series against the Suns, with the home team winning every game of the series so far. And unfortunately for the Mavs, the final game of the series would be held on the Suns' turf.

The atmosphere in Phoenix was electric before tip-off as the fans were eager to see their Suns team finally put the Mavericks to bed once and for all. But no one could have predicted the demolition job that the Mavericks would showcase against a Suns team that had dominated the NBA the entire season. Luka Doncic put up 35 points, 10 rebounds, and 4 assists in an all-around effort against the Suns to help the Mavericks advance to the Western Conference Finals for the first time since their championship run in 2011.

The Mavericks had exceeded all expectations by getting this far in the playoffs, and the team had all of the momentum it needed to keep on trudging toward a slot in the Finals. Unfortunately for the Mavericks, the eventual NBA champion Golden State Warriors proved to be too much for Doncic and the rest of the squad. The Warriors immediately shot out to a 3-0 series lead that effectively quashed the Mavericks' chances of getting back into the series. The Mavericks were able to eke out a win in Game 4 but were eventually put to rest by the Warriors in a series-clinching 120-110 loss in Game 5. Despite the losing effort,

Doncic still managed to get his usual spectacular numbers. He became the third player in NBA history to get 800 playoff career points within their first 25 playoff games. He also surpassed Mavericks legend Dirk Nowitzki for being the all-time franchise leader for 40+ point games in the playoffs.

Aside from pushing his team all the way to the Western Conference Finals, Doncic also bagged his third-straight All-NBA First Team award. He also finished fifth in MVP voting.

Chapter 5: What's Next for Luka?

Luka Doncic made history by signing a super-max rookie extension with the Mavs back before the start of the 2021-2022 NBA season. This came after a lot of speculation whether Doncic would even stay with the Mavericks once his rookie contract was up. But Doncic put all of those doubts to bed, and it looks like he'll be staying with Dallas for the foreseeable future after they agreed to pay him $207 million over five years. This is a lot of money to spend on a player who was barely 22 years old when he signed the deal. But Luka has already built the kind of career with groundbreaking records that many league veterans could never even dream of achieving.

In his first four years in the league, Doncic has already managed to become a three-time All-NBA First Team member, three-time NBA All-Star, Rookie of the Year, and he has managed to lead his team all the way to the Conference Finals. What's even more impressive is that he has managed to achieve all of this by the age of 23. Most NBA players typically reach their peak years at around their mid to late 20s, with many of them retiring during their mid to late 30s. And at the pace that Luka is going, it's almost scary to think what else he's going to accomplish as he works toward his peak.

One of the biggest criticisms that he had going into the previous season was whether he had what it takes to lead a team to winning in the playoffs. Everyone was already aware of his offensive prowess and his ability to dominate the game on his own. But many still questioned his value as a team player and whether his individual accolades could eventually translate into franchise wins. Luka put all of those doubts to bed by single-handedly carrying a Mavericks team without any other All-Stars to the Western Conference Finals after defeating the league-best Phoenix Suns in the second round. So, as far as that is concerned, Luka has proven his capabilities of leading a winning team.

However, another one of the big criticisms of his game is his ability to lock down opposing superstars. All throughout his career, many opposing coaches have used Doncic's liabilities on defense as a way to exploit the Mavericks. Many coaches developed gameplans that revolved around attacking Doncic directly on defense. Currently, Doncic still isn't the fastest or most athletic player in the league. That was also one of the reasons why he didn't end up getting picked higher for his draft class. This is one potential area of improvement that Doncic can work on as he progresses in his career. In the 2021-2022 season, Doncic achieved the lowest defensive rating for a season in his career at 106.5. His previous low defensive rating was during his rookie season when he was rated at 109.1. For context, the league average for defensive rating in the NBA was 112.5 during the 2021-2022 season. This placed Doncic just below average. And if he's going to become a superstar to the levels of legends like

Michael Jordan, Kobe Bryant, and LeBron James, he has to improve his defensive skills moving forward.

Lastly, while Luka already has a long list of awards and accolades that he has accumulated in his short career, there is always one particular milestone that all NBA greats are judged by: championships. Doncic was three wins away from playing in the NBA Finals in the previous season. The next logical step for his career would be to eventually lead the Mavericks into the finals and even potentially win a championship for them. Of course, this is a lot easier said than done as there are many NBA greats throughout history who have retired without getting any rings. For context, the Mavericks legend Dirk Nowitzki won his first and only championship with the Mavericks back in 2011. He was already 32 years old at that point and had been playing in the NBA for 13 years. Doncic has just turned 23 and is heading into his fifth year in the NBA.

Save for a few minor injuries here and there, Doncic has also been relatively healthy throughout his entire professional career. If he is able to stay healthy and continuously improve his game as he grows older, very few will doubt his ability to continue to shatter the record books and maybe even potentially win the elusive championship.

References

Aravantinos, D. (2018, January 25). *Story of the week: Luka Doncic through his mother's eyes!* Eurohoops. https://www.eurohoops.net/en/trademarks/601550/story-week-luka-doncic-mothers-eyes/

Dallas Mavericks. (n.d.). *Luka Doncic*. The Official Home of the Dallas Mavericks. Retrieved July 14, 2022, from https://www.mavs.com/team/roster/luka-doncic/

Garcia, J. (n.d.). *Luka Doncic | biography & wiki*. VAVEL. Retrieved July 14, 2022, from https://www.vavel.com/en-us/data/luka-doncic/bio/

Haislop, T. (2020, August 26). *NBA bubble, explained: A complete guide to the rules, teams, schedule & more for orlando games*. Www.sportingnews.com. https://www.sportingnews.com/us/nba/news/nba-bubble-rules-teams-schedule-orlando/zhap66a9hcwq1khmcex3ggabo

Luka Doncic. (n.d.). *My story*. Www.lukadoncic.com. https://www.lukadoncic.com/en/my-story

Wimbish, J. (2019, December 10). *Numbers don't lie: Luka doncic's historic sophomore season is second to none in the nba's modern era*. CBSSports.com. https://www.cbssports.com/nba/news/numbers-dont-lie-luka-doncics-historic-sophomore-season-is-second-to-none-in-the-nbas-modern-era/